A Mother's Prayer

For Her Children

By

Nancy Ann Yaeger

A Mother's Prayer For Her Children
by Nancy Ann Yaeger

ISBN 1-886513-76-7

Kirk House Publishers
PO Box 390759, Minneapolis, Minnesota 55439

Manufactured in the United States of America

**Dedicated to Daniel, Allison and Paul
-- my children for whom I pray daily.**

Preface

This unique book motivates you to specifically and intentionally pray for your children. God's inspired Word is the simple, perfect language to use in your daily prayers for your children. In **A Mother's Prayer**, each Scripture verse articulates the exact Godly characteristic you yearn for your children to develop; each heartfelt prayer echoes God's powerful Word.

While set on the kitchen window sill or computer desk to be frequently seen throughout the day, not only will you pray often for your children, but you will also easily memorize the Scripture and firmly fix each verse into your own heart and mind. As a result, your faith is nourished and strengthened.

A Mother's Prayer provides 216 Bible verses and prayers. Your pace is your own. If you choose to focus on a specific virtue for some time, you cannot "fall behind". As a result, you can learn God's character and promises. Pray God's word for your children and live God's word in faith.

"I have no greater joy than this, to hear that
my children are walking in the truth."
3 John 4 NRSV

Diligent

"You have commanded your precepts to be kept diligently."

Psalm 119:4

May my children diligently keep your Word, O Lord. Amen.

Worthy

"Only, live your life in a manner worthy of the gospel of Christ."

Philippians 1:27(a)

Lord Jesus, may my children live their life in a manner worthy of the gospel. Amen.

Faithful

"Be faithful until death, and I will give you the crown of life."

Revelation 2:10(b)

Jesus, keep my children faithful so that at their death they may receive the crown of life. Amen.

Holy

"You must be holy, because I am holy."
1 Peter 1:16

Holy God, fill my children with the desire to be holy as you are holy. Amen.

Pursue Peace

"Let us then pursue what makes for peace and for mutual upbuilding."
Romans 14:19

Almighty God, may my children pursue those activities that make for peace and for mutual upbuilding. Amen.

Joyful

"Make a joyful noise to God, all the earth; sing the glory of his name; give to him glorious praise."

Psalm 66:1

May my children make a joyful noise to you, O God, and sing the glory of your name. Amen.

Imitators

"Be imitators of God."
Ephesians 5:1(a)

Holy God, may I set an example for my children so they may be imitators of your love as Christ loved us. Amen.

Watchful

"Keep a close watch on all you do and think. Stay true to what is right and God will bless you and use you to help others."

1 Timothy 4:16

Savior, keep my children watchful for spiritual danger, firm in the faith, courageous to do what is right and strong to resist temptation. Amen.

Gracious

"Let your speech always be gracious, seasoned with salt, so that you may know how you ought to answer everyone."
Colossians 4:6

Help my children, O Lord, speak graciously as well as sensibly, that they may have the right answers for everyone. Amen.

Content

"Keep your lives free from the love of money and be content with what you have, because God has said, 'Never will I leave you; never will I forsake you.'"
Hebrews 13:5

Heavenly Father, whether we have much or little, help our family to be content with what we have knowing that you are with us always. Amen.

Happy

"Happy are those who trust in the Lord."

Proverbs 16:20(b)

Lord, may my children's trust in you bring happiness to their lives. Amen.

Wisdom

"If any of you lacks wisdom, he should ask God, who gives generously to all without finding fault, and it will be given to him."
James 1:5

Lord, I pray for wisdom to raise my children and wisdom for my children to discern your ways. Amen.

Forgiving

"If someone does wrong to you, forgive that person because the Lord forgave you."

Colossians 3:13(b)

Lord, teach my children to forgive as you have forgiven us. Amen.

Wait Expectantly

"I wait for the Lord, my soul waits, and in his word I put my hope."

Psalm 130:5

Sovereign Lord, may my children wait expectantly for answers to their prayers knowing your word is truth and your perfect ways are not our ways. Amen.

Thankful

"It is good to give thanks to the Lord, to sing praises to your name, O Most High; to declare your steadfast love in the morning, and your faithfulness by night."
>
> Psalm 92:1-2

May my children be ever thankful, Lord, to sing praises to your name from morning until night. Amen.

Integrity

"He who walks in integrity walks securely."
Proverbs 10:9(a)

Father, help my children walk in integrity knowing their life is secure in you. Amen.

Merciful

"Blessed are the merciful, for they will receive mercy."
Matthew 5:7

Lord, help my children comprehend your mercy so that they may be merciful to others. Amen.

Boastful in the Lord

"Let the one who boasts, boast in the Lord."
2 Corinthians 10:17

Grant, Lord, that my children will know that all things come from you and so only boast in the Lord. Amen.

Peacemaker

"Blessed are the peacemakers, for they will be called children of God."

Matthew 5:9

Father, in this conflicted world may my children be at peace with the knowledge of your love and thereby be peacemakers among all people. Amen.

Courage

"Be strong, and let your heart take courage, all you who wait for the Lord."

Psalm 31:24

Lord, help my children be strong and let their hearts take courage as they stand firm in their hope in you. Amen.

Non-judgmental

"...for at whatever point you judge the other, you are condemning yourself, because you who pass judgment do the same things."

Romans 2:1

Heavenly Father, help me teach my children not to judge others but rather to love as you have loved us. Amen.

Openhanded to Poor

"Do not be hardhearted or tightfisted toward your poor brother. Rather be openhanded and freely lend him whatever he needs."
Deuteronomy 15:7(b)-8

Father, keep my children from being hardhearted or tightfisted toward the poor; lead them to be openhanded and freely lend to those in need. Amen.

Alert

"Be self-controlled and alert. Your enemy the devil prowls around like a roaring lion looking for someone to devour."

1 Peter 5:8

Keep my children alert, O Lord, that they may recognize and resist the devil and his evil ways. Amen.

Prepared

"Always be prepared to give an answer to everyone who asks you to give the reason for the hope that you have."

1 Peter 3:15

Lord Jesus, I pray for my children to have a rock solid foundation in your Word that they will be prepared to enlighten others who question their hope in you. Amen.

Blameless

"Do everything without complaining or arguing, so that you may become blameless and pure, children of God..."
Philippians 2:14-15(a)

God, help me to teach my children to become blameless and pure by not complaining or arguing. Amen.

Competent

"Not that we are competent in ourselves to claim anything for ourselves, but our competence comes from God."
2 Corinthians 3:5(b)

Almighty God, give my children competence to use their talents in ministry to you. Amen.

Zealous

"Never be lacking in zeal, but keep your spiritual fervor, serving the Lord."
Romans 12:11

May my children be zealous to your calling, O Lord. Amen.

Hospitable

"Offer hospitality to one
another with out grumbling."
1 Peter 4:9

**Jesus, inspire us to offer hospitality to
all people so we may reflect your love.
Amen.**

Spotless

"Make every effort to be found spotless, blameless, and at peace with (God)."
2 Peter 3:14

Help me, Lord, to encourage my children to make every effort to be found spotless, blameless, and at peace. Amen.

Humble

"And all of you must clothe yourselves with humility in your dealings with one another, for 'God opposes the proud but gives grace to the humble.'"

1 Peter 5:5(b)

Dear God, clothe my children with humility in their dealings with one another. Amen.

Beautiful

"It is not fancy hair, gold jewelry, or fine clothes that should make you beautiful. No your beauty should come from within you – the beauty of a gentle and quiet spirit that will never be destroyed and is very precious to God."
1 Peter 3:3-5

God our Creator, help me to teach my children that true beauty is not the physical beauty portrayed on T.V. and the movies but rather the inner beauty of a gentle and quiet spirit filled with your love. Amen.

Directed

"May the Lord direct your hearts to the love of God and to the steadfastness of Christ."
2 Thessalonians 3:5

Lord God, direct my children's hearts to your love and to an unwavering faith in Christ. Amen.

Standing Firm

"He who stands firm to the end will be saved."
Matthew 24:13

Lord, keep my children standing firm in their faith until the end of time. Amen.

Worshipful

"Come, let us bow down in worship, let us kneel before the Lord our Maker."
Psalm 95:6

Lord our Maker, may my children bow down to worship you each day. Amen.

Shielded by God's Power

"Through faith [we] are shielded by God's power until the coming of the salvation that is ready to be revealed in the last time."

1 Peter 1:5

Lord God, through my children's faith shield them by your power until you come again. Amen.

Matched with Believers

"Do not be mismatched with unbelievers. For what partnership is there between righteousness and lawlessness? Or what does a believer share with an unbeliever."

2 Corinthians 6:14

Jesus, I pray for my children's future mates that they know, love, and follow you always. Amen.

Restored

"Restore me, and I will return, because you are the Lord my God."

Jeremiah 31:18

Restore my children, Lord, that they may be refreshed with your love and cling to you. Amen.

Overcome Unbelief

"I do believe; help me over-
come my unbelief."
Mark 9:24

**Jesus, when doubts assail my children
may they call out to you for help
saying, "I believe, help my unbelief."
Amen.**

Do All Things Through Christ

"I can do all things through Christ because he gives me strength."

Philippians 4:13

Dear Jesus, give my children the understanding that they can do everything within your will through your strength and power. Amen.

Commit

"Commit everything you do to the Lord. Trust him to help you do it and he will."
Psalm 37:5

Lord, help my children commit everything they do to you and to trust you to help them do it. Amen.

Child-like Faith

"Let the little children come to me! Never send them away! For the Kingdom of God belongs to men who have hearts as trusting as these little children's."

Luke 18:16

Lord Jesus, as my children mature, maintain their child-like trust and faith in you. Amen.

Joyful

"Restore to me the joy of your salvation, and sustain me with a willing spirit."
Psalm 51:12

Lord, give to my children the joy of your salvation and a willingness to obey you. Amen.

Perseverance

"... Let us run with perseverance the race marked out for us. Let us fix our eyes on Jesus, the author and perfecter of our faith..."
Hebrews 12:1(a)-2(b)

Jesus, strengthen my children to run with perseverance life's race toward you, always keeping you in their sight. Amen.

Integrity

"I know, my God, that you test the heart and are pleased with integrity."

1 Chronicles 29:17

Holy God, cultivate integrity within my children so when you test their hearts you will be pleased. Amen.

Own Understanding

"Trust in the Lord with all your heart and lean not on your own understanding."
Proverbs 3:5

Lord Jesus, guide my children to depend not on their own understanding and wisdom but to trust in you with all their heart. Amen.

Confess

"So that every knee will bow to the name of Jesus– everyone, in heaven, on earth, and under the earth. And everyone will confess that Jesus Christ is Lord, and bring glory to God the Father."

Philippians 2:10-11

Jesus, may my children bow down and confess that you are Lord and bring glory to you. Amen.

Pure

"For God wants you to be holy and pure, and to keep clear of all sexual sin so that each of you will marry in holiness and honor."

1 Thessalonians 4:3-4

God, keep my children holy and pure that they may enter marriage in holiness and honor. Amen.

Crowned with Success

"In everything you do put God first, and he will direct you and crown your efforts with success."

Proverbs 3:6

Lord God, in everything my children do guide them to put you first, direct them in the way they should go, and crown their efforts with success. Amen.

Good

"Seek good, not evil, that you may live."

Amos 5:14

Lord, encourage my children to seek good, not evil, that they may live with you forever. Amen.

Controlled Tongue

"For by your words you will be justified, and by your words you will be condemned."

Matthew 12:37

Teach my children to glorify you with their mouths and to keep control over their tongues. Amen.

Alive in Christ

"I know your works; you have a name of being alive, but you are dead. Wake up, and strengthen what remains . . ."
Revelation 3:1-2(a)

Heavenly Father, help my children be alive in Christ in both name and works. Keep them awake to your gracious love. Amen.

Witness

"You will be my witness . . .to the ends of the earth."
Acts 1:8

Father, may my children be a witness for you all the days of their lives. Amen.

Conquerors

"If you conquer, you will be clothed like them in white robes, and I will not blot your name out of the book of life; I will confess your name before my Father and before his angels."
Revelation 3:5

Father, I pray that my children will be conquerors of the faith who will someday hear their name confessed before you. Amen.

Ambassador

"So we are ambassadors for Christ, since God is making his appeal through us."
2 Corinthians 5:20

Almighty God, help my children be ambassadors for Christ, clarifying your will to an estranged world. Amen.

Hot Faith

"I know what you do, that you are not hot or cold. I wish that you were hot or cold!"
Revelation 3:15

Lord, I pray that my children's faith will be red hot for you so their works will bring praises to you. Amen.

Assurance

"I want their hearts to be encouraged and united in love, so that they may have all the riches of assured understanding and have the knowledge of God's mystery, that is, Christ himself, in whom are hidden all the treasures of wisdom and knowledge."

Colossians 2:2

Father, may my children have full assurance of your salvation through Christ Jesus. Amen.

Believe

"Believe on the Lord Jesus, and you will be saved, you and your household."
Acts 16:31

Help my children to believe, Lord. Amen.

Delight

"I delight to do your will, O my God; your law is within my heart."

Psalm 40:8

O God, may my children delight to do your will. Amen.

Grow in Grace

"But grow in the grace and knowledge of our Lord and Savior Jesus Christ."
2 Peter 3:18

The seed of faith has been planted, Lord. Please help it grow in the grace and knowledge of Jesus. Amen.

Good Deeds

"Show yourself in all respects
a model of good deeds. . ."
Titus 2:7(a)

O God, inspire my children to be a
model of good deeds to reflect your
love. Amen.

Cheerful

"For God loves a cheerful giver."

2 Corinthians 9:7(b)

Sovereign Lord, motivate my children to have an attitude of gratitude and be a cheerful giver. Amen.

Eagerly Waiting

"So Christ, having been offered once to bear the sins of many, will appear a second time, not to deal with sin, but to save those who are eagerly waiting for him."
Hebrews 9:28

Jesus, my Savior, when you come again may you find my children eagerly waiting for you. Amen.

Choose

"You must choose for yourselves today whom you will serve. . . As for me and my family, we will serve the Lord."

Joshua 24:15

Almighty God, may my children choose to serve you. Amen.

Ask, Seek, Knock

"Ask, and it will be given you; seek, and you will find; knock, and the door will be opened for you."

Matthew 7:7

Lord, help my children to rely on you and to ask, seek, and knock. Amen.

Ears that Listen

"Let anyone with ears listen!"
Matthew 11:15

Lord, open my children's ears so they
will listen to you. Amen.

Encourage

"Therefore encourage one another and build up each other."

1 Thessalonians 5:11

Heavenly Father, help my children to encourage one another and build up each other. Amen.

Rooted in Love

"And I pray that you, being rooted and established in love, may have power, together with all the saints, to grasp how wide and long and high and deep is the love of Christ."

Ephesians 3:17-18(a)

Jesus, I pray that my children, being rooted and established in love, will have the power to grasp how wide and long and high and deep is your love. Amen.

Knowledge of His Will

"We have not stopped praying for
you and asking God to fill you with
the knowledge of his will, through all
spiritual wisdom and understanding
... that you may live a life worthy of
the Lord and may please him in every
way; bearing fruit in every good
work, growing in the knowledge of
God."   Colossians 1:9-10

**O God, fill my children with knowledge of
your will for their lives that they may lead
a life worthy of you by bearing fruit in
every good work. Amen.**

Calls on the Lord

"Anyone who calls on the
Lord will be saved."
Romans 10:13

**Lord, arouse my children to call upon
your name and be saved. Amen.**

Proclaim

"For as often as you eat this bread and drink the cup, you proclaim the Lord's death until he comes."

1 Corinthians 11:26

Lord Jesus, stir up the desire within my children to frequently come to your table to proclaim and retell the message of your victory over death. Amen.

Clings to the Lord

"My soul clings to you; your
right hand upholds me."
Psalm 63:8

Lord Jesus, may my children's souls
cling to you; may your right hand
uphold them. Amen.

Compassion

"As God's chosen ones, holy and beloved, clothe yourselves with compassion, kindness, humility, meekness, and patience."

Colossians 3:12

O God, clothe my children in compassion, kindness, humility, meekness and patience. Amen.

Not Proud

"So do not become proud, but stand in awe."

Romans 11:20(b)

Keep my children from being proud for all they have and do. May they stand in awe of you, Lord, and give you the glory for their riches. Amen.

Spirit-filled

"Do not quench the Spirit."
1 Thessalonians 5:19

Holy Spirit, dwell in my children's hearts; help them not quench the Spirit. Amen.

Meek

"Blessed are the meek, for they will inherit the earth."
Matthew 5:5

Lord, may my children be meek so they will inherit the earth. Amen.

Stand Mature

"Stand mature and fully assured in everything that God wills."

Colossians 4:12(b)

Help my children stand mature and fully assured in your will, O God. Amen.

Christian

"Yet if any of you suffers as a Christian, do not consider it a disgrace, but glorify God because you bear this name."
1 Peter 4:16

Lord Jesus, let us not be ashamed that we are Christians but rather stand firm and glorify you. Amen.

Not Greedy

"Beware! Don't be greedy for what you don't have. Real life is not measure by how much we own."

Luke 12:15

Creator God, guard my children from wishing for what they don't have and teach them that real life is not valued by our earthly possessions. Amen.

Sufficient Grace

"My grace is sufficient for you, for my power is made perfect in weakness."

2 Corinthians 12:9

Grant that my children will understand that all they really need is your grace and that through their weakness your power is revealed. Amen.

Dependent on God

"When you bow down before the Lord and admit your dependence on him, he will lift you up and give you honor."

James 4:10

Make us dependent on you, Lord, that you may lift us up and give us honor. Amen.

Know Right from Wrong

"For I want you always to see clearly the difference between right and wrong, and to be inwardly clean, no one being able to criticize you from now until our Lord returns."

Philippians 1:10

Father, I pray that my children always see clearly the difference between right and wrong, and are inwardly clean so no one can criticize them. Amen.

Crave God's Word

"Like new born babies, crave pure spiritual milk, so that by it you may grow up in your salvation."

1 Peter 2:2

Lord Jesus, may my children crave to study your Word that they may grow up in their salvation. Amen.

Doing Good

"May you always be doing those good, kind things which show that you are a child of God, for this will bring much praise and glory to the Lord."
Philippians 1:11

Jesus, help my children do those good, kind things which show they are your children and thereby bring praise and glory to you. Amen.

Silence Ignorant Talk

"For it is God's will that by doing good you should silence the ignorant talk of foolish men."

1 Peter 2:15

Lord Jesus, when my children's faith is challenged by people who resist reading your Word may you give them strength to do good and thereby silence the ignorant talk of foolish men. Amen.

Servant Leader

"Whoever wants to become great among you must serve the rest of you like a servant."
Matthew 20:26(b)

Savior, teach my children, as you did your disciples, that if they want to be a leader they must act like a servant and lead by serving the needs of others. Amen.

Reverent Fear

"[God] will judge you with perfect justice for everything you do; so act in reverent fear of him from now on until you get to heaven."
1 Peter 1:17

Dear God, grant that my children will understand your perfect justice prevails so they live their lives in reverent fear and awe of you from now until they get to heaven. Amen.

Live in Harmony

"Finally, all of you, live in harmony with one another; be sympathetic, love as brothers, be compassionate and humble."
1 Peter 3:8

Jesus, my Savior, teach my children to live in harmony with each other by being sympathetic, loving, compassionate and humble. Amen.

Overflow with Love

"My prayer for you is that you will overflow more and more with love for others, and at the same time keep on growing in spiritual knowledge and insight." Philippians 1:9

Dear God, my prayer echoes your inspired words that my children will overflow with love for others and at the same time keep on growing in spiritual knowledge and insight. Amen.

Understand God's Will

"Therefore do not be foolish,
but understand what the
Lord's will is."

Ephesians 5:17

O God, keep my children from
foolishness and inspire them to read
your Word so they understand your
will. Amen.

Understand Wages of Sin

"For the wages of sin is death, but the free gift of God is eternal life in Christ Jesus our Lord."

Romans 6:23

Christ Jesus, help my children understand that the wages of sin is death, but through faith in you they have the free gift of eternal life. Amen.

Walk in Truth

"Teach me your way, O Lord,
and I will walk in your truth."
Psalm 86:11

**O Lord, teach my children your way
so they will walk in your truth. Amen.**

Abide in Christ

"And now, little children, abide in him, so that when he is revealed we may have confidence and not be put to shame before him at his coming."

1 John 2:28

Dear Jesus, may my children abide in you so that when you come again they may stand confidently and say "Here I am Lord, I'm ready for you." Amen.

Know Truth

"If you continue in my word, you are truly my disciples; and you will know the truth, and the truth will make you free."
John 8:31(b)-32

Lord Jesus, with so much confusion in this world help my children learn what is true by studying your Word and living according to your Truth. Amen.

Doing Right

"So let us not grow weary in doing what is right, for we will reap at harvest time, if we do not give up."

Galatians 6:9

Lord Jesus, strengthen my children so they will not grow weary in doing right. Amen.

Victory

"But thanks be to God, who always leads us in victory through Christ."
2 Corinthians 2:14(a)

Holy God, thanks be to you for leading my children in victory over sin and worldly temptations. Amen.

Trained in Godliness

"Train yourself in godliness."
1 Timothy 4:7(b)

Dear Jesus, help my children to train themselves in godliness and uphold your values. Amen.

Confess

"I said, 'I will confess my sins to the Lord' -- and you forgave my guilt."
Psalm 32:5(b)

When my children do wrong, Lord, may they confess their sins and receive your forgiveness. Amen.

Outcome of Faith

"For you are receiving the outcome of your faith, the salvation of your souls."
1 Peter 1:9

Thank you God for the promise that the outcome of our faith is the salvation of our souls. May my children praise you for their faith and salvation. Amen.

Strong

"Be strong in the faith, just as you were taught, and always be thankful."

Colossians 2:7(b)

Dear Lord, keep my children strong in the faith, just as they were taught, and always be thankful. Amen.

Good Stewards

"Like good stewards of the manifold grace of God, serve one another with whatever gift each of you has received."
1 Peter 4:10

Help me teach my children to be good stewards with the special abilities and gifts you give to each one. Amen.

Humility

"Show true humility to everyone."
Titus 3:2(b)

O Lord, grant that my children show true humility toward all people. Amen.

Sincere Heart

"Let us draw near to God with a sincere heart in full assurance of faith."
                    Hebrews 10:22

Help my children draw near to you with a sincere heart in full assurance of faith. Amen.

No Evil Talk

"Let no evil talk come out of your mouths, but only what is useful for building up, as there is need, so that your words may give grace to those who hear."

Ephesians 4:29

Lord Jesus, let no evil talk come out of my children's mouths. Amen.

Accepting of Others

"Christ accepted you so you should accept each other, which will bring glory to God."

Romans 15:7

Through your example Jesus, teach us to accept and welcome others regardless of who they are or what they might have done so we maintain Christian unity. Amen.

Meditate

"His delight is in the law of the Lord, and on his law he meditates day and night."
Psalm 1:2

May my children meditate on your Word, O Lord, day and night. Amen.

God's Will

"Be joyful always; pray continually; give thanks in all circumstances, for this is God's will for you in Christ Jesus."
1 Thessalonians 5:16-18

Lord Jesus, in a world abounding in confusion, may my children understand your will is for them to be joyful, prayerful, and thankful at all times. Amen.

Endurance

"By your endurance you will gain your souls."
Luke 21:19

Jesus, when my children are teased and persecuted for their faith assure them that by their endurance they will gain salvation. Amen.

Bold

"Let us therefore approach the throne of grace with boldness, so that we may receive mercy and find grace to help in time of need."

Hebrews 4:16

Almighty Lord, with boldness let my children draw near to receive your mercy and find grace to help in time of need. Amen.

Clean Heart

"Create in me a clean heart, O God. Renew a right spirit within me."

Psalm 51:10

Create in me and my children a clean heart, O God, and renew a right spirit within us. Amen.

Way Out/Endurance

"God is faithful, and he will not let you be tested beyond your strength, but with testing he will also provide the way out so that you may be able to endure it."

1 Corinthians 10:13

Faithful Lord, when my children are tempted, show them the way out so they may be able to endure it. Amen.

Shine

"Let your light shine before others, so that they may see your good works and give glory to your Father in heaven."

Matthew 5:16

Let my children's light so shine before all people, O God, that all may see their good works and give glory to you. Amen.

Eternal Life

"Lord, to whom can we go? You have the words of eternal life."
John 6:68

Lord, you have the words of eternal life. Help my children to believe. Amen.

Fruit of the Spirit

"By contrast, the fruit of the Spirit is love, joy, peace, patience, kindness, generosity, faithfulness, gentleness, and self-control."
Galatians 5:22-23(a)

O God, fill my children with the fruit of the Spirit. May they show love, joy, peace, patience, kindness, generosity, faithfulness, gentleness, and self-control. Amen.

Righteousness of God

"For our sake he made him to be sin who knew no sin, so that in him we might become the righteousness of God."

2 Corinthians 5:21

Thank you God for pouring our sins into your sinless son, Jesus, and in exchange pouring your righteousness into us. Amen.

Fulfilled

"The Lord will fulfill his purpose for me."
Psalm 138:8

Lord, we know that you will fulfill your purpose for us. Amen.

Love

"Love is patient; love is kind; love is
not envious or boastful or arrogant or
rude. It does not insist on its own
way; it is not irritable or resentful; it
does not rejoice in wrongdoing, but
rejoices in the truth. It bears all
things, believes all things, hopes all
things, endures all things."
1 Corinthians 13:4-7

**Lord God, help my children learn the
true meaning of love and may they
learn it through my example. Amen.**

Glad

"I was glad when they said to me, 'Let us go to the house of the Lord!'"

Psalm 122:1

Lord, I pray that my children will be glad to go to church to worship you. Amen.

Insight

"The fear of the Lord is the beginning of wisdom, and the knowledge of the Holy One is insight."

Proverbs 9:10

Lord, grant my children insight and knowledge of your holiness. Amen.

Good

"We know that all things work together for good for those who love God, who are called according to his purpose."
Romans 8:28

God, when my children run into disappointments may they be assured by the knowledge that in everything you work for good with those who love you, and are living according to your purpose. Amen.

Confess

"If you confess with your lips that Jesus is Lord and believe in your heart that God raised him from the dead, you will be saved."

Romans 10:9

Holy God, may my children confess with their lips that Jesus is Lord and believe in their hearts that you raised Jesus from the dead, so they will be saved. Amen.

Listening

"This is my beloved Son, and I am fully pleased with him; Listen to him."

Matthew 17:5(b)

Almighty Lord, help my children to listen to your beloved Son as they hear your Word. Amen.

Mustard Seed Faith

"... if you have faith as small as a mustard seed... nothing will be impossible for you."
Matthew 17:20

Jesus, my Savior, grant that my children may have faith at least the size of a mustard seed. Amen.

Day of Salvation

"See, now is the day of
salvation!"
2 Corinthians 6:2(b)

**God, right now you are ready to
welcome us. Guide my children to
choose the salvation you offer without
delay for now is the day of salvation.
Amen.**

Life

"God has given us eternal life, and this life is in his Son. He who has the Son has life; he who does not have the Son of God does not have life."
1 John 5:11-12

Holy God, you have given us eternal life. Help my children believe in your Son so they may have life. Amen.

Know God

"Be still and know that I am God."

Psalm 46:10

God Almighty, help my children find quiet times to be still and know that you are our God. Amen.

Press On

"I press on toward the goal for the prize of the heavenly call of God in Christ Jesus."
Philippians 3:14

Jesus, help my children press on to that heavenly goal to be with you and to follow your call. Amen.

Gentleness

"Let your gentleness be evident to all."
Philippians 4:5

Lord, let my children's gentleness be evident so everyone may see that they are unselfish and considerate in all they do. Amen.

No Condemnation

"Therefore, there is now no condemnation for those who are in Christ Jesus."

Romans 8:1

What joy, O Lord, for my children to know there is now no condemnation for those who are in Christ Jesus. Amen.

Justified

"Therefore, since we are justified by faith, we have peace with God through our Lord Jesus Christ."
                    Romans 5:1

May my children have peace knowing they are justified by faith in Jesus Christ. Amen.

Living Sacrifice

".... in view of God's mercy ... offer your bodies as living sacrifices, holy and pleasing to God."

Romans 12:1

Lord Jesus, may my children's bodies be holy and pleasing to you. Amen.

Ready

"Therefore you also must be ready, for the Son of Man is coming at an unexpected hour."

Matthew 24:44

Keep my children ever ready to meet you face-to-face, O Lord. Amen.

Hunger and Thirst for Righteousness

"Blessed are those who hunger and thirst for righteousness, for they will be filled."
Matthew 5:6

God grant my children a true hunger for your Word and a desire to be just and good. Amen.

Redemption

"In him we have redemption through his blood, the forgiveness of our sins in accordance with the riches of God's grace."

Ephesians 1:7

Lord Jesus, thank you for the redemption we have through your death and resurrection. Amen.

Safe

"If you trust in the Lord, you will be safe."

Proverbs 29:25(b)

Help my children find safety in trusting you, Almighty God.

Pure in Heart

"Blessed are the pure in heart, for they will see God."
Matthew 5:8

God, help my children be pure in heart so they will see you. Amen.

Righteous

"The righteous will live by faith."

Romans 1:17(b)

Grant, O God, that my children will live by faith and be righteous. Amen.

Devoted to Prayer

"Devote yourselves to prayer, being watchful and thankful." Colossians 4:2

Lord Jesus, may my children devote themselves to prayer, being watchful for your answers and thankful for your blessings. Amen.

Whole Armor

"Put on the whole armor of God, so that you may be able to stand against the wiles of the devil."

Ephesians 6:11

God, clothe my children with your armor that they may withstand the wiles of the devil. Amen.

The Way

"Jesus answered, 'I am the way, the truth, and the life." John 14:6

Jesus, grant my children the knowledge that you are the way and the truth and the giver of life eternal. Amen.

Completed Good Work

"I am confident of this, that the one who began a good work among you will bring it to completion by the day of Jesus Christ."

Philippians 1:6

Lord Jesus, give my children the confidence to know that you, who began a good work in them, will bring it to completion and keep on helping them grow in your grace until you come again. Amen.

Stand Straight

"So when all these things begin to happen, stand straight and look up! For your salvation is near."

Luke 21:28

Lord, when the end of the age is near may my children stand straight and look for you knowing their salvation is near. Amen.

Judge Not

"Do not judge, so that you
may not be judged."
Matthew 7:1

Lord, help my children see their own
sin before pointing out the sins of
others. Amen.

Sow Generously

"Remember this: Whoever sows sparingly will also reap sparingly, and whoever sows generously will also reap generously."

2 Corinthians 9:6

Lord Jesus, help my children understand that the more they give the more you give them what they need, so that those helped will praise you. Amen.

Build-Pray-Keep

"But you, beloved, build
yourselves up on your most holy
faith; pray in the Holy Spirit; keep
yourselves in the love of God;
look forward to the mercy of our
Lord Jesus Christ that leads to
eternal life."

Jude 20-21

**God, may my children build on the
foundation of their faith, pray in the
power of the Holy Spirit, keep in your
love, and wait patiently for eternal
life. Amen.**

Trust

"I trust in God's unfailing love
for ever and ever."
Psalm 52:8

I pray, dear God, that my children
will trust in your unfailing love for
ever and ever. Amen.

Suffer for God

". . . rejoicing that God had counted them worthy to suffer dishonor for his name."
Acts 5:41

May my children rejoice in the honor to suffer for you. Amen.

Work Hard

"Work hard and cheerfully at all you do, just as though you were working for the Lord and not merely for your masters."
Colossians 3:23

Help my children, Lord, to work hard as though serving you and not merely for others. Amen.

Submit to God

"Submit yourselves therefore to God. Resist the devil, and he will flee from you."
James 4:7

Almighty God, may my children submit themselves to you and resist the devil. Amen.

Give Thanks

"O give thanks to the Lord, for he is good, for his steadfast love endures forever."
Psalm 106:1

May my children give thanks, O Lord, for you are good and your steadfast love endures for ever. Amen.

Transformed

"Do not be conformed to this world, but be transformed by the renewing of your minds, so that you may discern what is the will of God– what is good and acceptable and perfect."
Romans 12:2

Almighty God, when my children are faced with peer pressure to do what they know is wrong, give them the strength to resist and not conform but be transformed to do what is good and acceptable and perfect. Amen.

Treasures in Heaven

"Do not lay up for yourselves treasures on earth... but lay up for yourselves treasures in heaven... For where your treasure is there will your heart be also."

Matthew 6:19-21

Dear Jesus, as the materialism of this world vies for my children's attention, grant them strength to focus on the treasures of heaven. Amen.

Rejoice

"Rejoice in the Lord always;
again I will say, Rejoice."
Philippians 4:4

**Lord, may my children always be full
of joy in you and rejoice. Amen.**

Seek

"But seek first his kingdom and his righteousness, and all these things will be given to you as well."
Matthew 6:33

Lord God, guide my children to seek first your kingdom and righteousness in their lives. Amen.

Perfect

"Be perfect, therefore, as your heavenly Father is perfect."
Matthew 5:48

Teach us all to be perfect as you are perfect, Heavenly Father. Amen.

Provided in Abundance

"And God is able to provide you with every blessing in abundance, so that by always having enough of everything, you may share abundantly in every good work."

2 Corinthians 9:8

God of all goodness, give an understanding to my children that you provide them with all they need and more so they may joyfully provide for the needs of others in return. Amen.

No Room for
the Devil

"And do not make room for the devil."

Ephesians 4:27

**Keep my children safe from giving the devil any opportunity to do evil.
Amen.**

Praise

"Praise the Lord, O my soul."
Psalm 104:35

May my children's souls sing praises to you, O Lord. Amen.

Strength in God

"God is our refuge and strength, a very present help in trouble."
                    Psalm 46:1

May my children depend on you, O God, as their refuge and strength in times of trouble. Amen.

New Creation

"So if any one is in Christ, there is a new creation: everything has become new!"
2 Corinthians 5:17

May my children be a new creation in Christ, O Lord. Amen.

God's Plan

"For I know the plans I have for you, says the Lord. 'They are plans for good and not for disaster, to give you a future and a hope.'"

Jeremiah 29:11

Lord, instill in my children the peace that comes from knowing that you have a plan for their future. Amen.

Neighborly

"Love does no wrong to a neighbor."

Romans 13:10(a)

Teach my children to love their neighbor as they love themselves so they do no wrong to their neighbors. Amen.

Image of God

"So God created human beings in his image. In the image of God he created them. He created them male and female."
                    Genesis 1:27

Almighty God and Creator, help my children comprehend that you created them in your image. Amen.

Obedient

"This is love for God; to obey
his commands."
1 John 5:3

God help my children show their love
for you by obeying your commandments. Amen.

Honor Parents

"Honor your father and your mother, so that your days may be long in the land that the Lord your God is giving you."
Exodus 20:12

May my children remember your command, Lord, to honor their parents that they may have a long life. Amen.

Move

"In him we live and move and have our being."

Acts 17:28(a)

Lord, grant that my children are so much a part of you that they may proclaim, 'In him we live and move and have our being.' Amen.

Salt

"You are the salt of the earth."
Matthew 5:13

**Jesus, make my children the salt of
the earth, sprinkling your love on all
the world. Amen.**

Fellow Citizen

"Consequently, you are no longer foreigners and aliens, but fellow citizens with God's people and members of God's household."

Ephesians 2:19

We praise you God that we are not foreigners wandering aimlessly, but rather fellow citizens with your people and members of your household. Amen.

Light

"You are the light of the
world."

Matthew 5:14

**Lord may my children be a bright
light that all the world may see their
good deeds to bring praises to you.
Amen.**

Kind

"Be kind and loving to each other, and forgive each other, just as God forgave you."
Ephesians 4:32

Jesus, help my children to be kind to one another. Amen.

Mature

"Don't be childish in your understanding of these things. Be innocent as babies when it come to evil, but be mature and wise in understanding matters of this kind."
1 Corinthians 14:20

Mighty God, may my children become mature Christians in their thinking. Amen.

Inspired

"All scripture is inspired by God and profitable for teaching, for reproof, for correction, and for training in righteousness, that people of God may be complete, equipped for every good work."
2 Timothy 3:16

God, help my children grasp that the words of the Bible come from you as you inspired people to write down your will so that we can use your truths for living our life. Amen.

Pure Mind

"Set your minds on things above, not on earthly things."
Colossians 3:2

Lord, help my children focus on things with a heavenly value, not on things of earthly value. Amen.

Just

"The Lord is just in all his ways, and kind in all his doings."

Psalm 145:17

Lord, may we strive to be just and kind in all we do. Amen.

Heavens

"When I look at your heavens,
the work of your fingers, the
moon and the stars that you
have established; what are
human beings that you are
mindful of them, and mortals
that you care for them?"
                    Psalm 8:3-4

**Heavenly Father, when we see the
majesty of your universe may we
praise you that you care for and love
us. Amen.**

Hope

"But blessed are those who trust in the Lord and have made the Lord their hope and confidence."

Jeremiah 17:7

Almighty God, I pray that you will be my children's hope and confidence. Amen.

Heart and Soul

"Love the Lord your God with all your heart, all your soul, all your strength, and all your mind."

Luke 10:27(a)

Lord my God, I pray that my children will love you with all of their heart, soul, strength, and mind. Amen.

Gain

"For to me, living is Christ, and dying is gain."
                    Philippians 1:21

Lord Jesus, help my children understand that to live gives us serving opportunities for you and to die means coming into your presence which is better yet. Amen.

Knowledge

"The fear of the Lord is the beginning of knowledge."
Proverbs 1:7

Lord, may my children have a profound reverence for you. Amen.

Glory

"The heavens are telling the glory of God; and the firmament proclaims his handiwork."

Psalm 19:1

Almighty God, when my children see your creation all around them may they see your glory and give you thanks. Amen.

Keep the Faith

"I have fought the good fight, I have finished the race, I have kept the faith."

2 Timothy 4:7

Almighty God, at the end of our lives may we be able to say I have fought the good fight, I have finished the race, I have kept the faith. Amen.

Sharing

"I pray that you may be active in sharing your faith, so that you will have a full understanding of every good thing we have in Christ."
Philemon 1:6

Christ Jesus, I pray that my children may be active in sharing their faith and come to understand all the good that is theirs in you. Amen.

Examined

"Let us test and examine our ways, and return to the Lord."
Lamentations 3:40

Lord, let my children test and examine their ways so if they have strayed they may return to you. Amen.

Example

"Set the believers an example in speech and conduct, in love, in faith, in purity."

1 Timothy 4:12

Lord Jesus, you are our example to follow. May my children set an example in speech, in life, in love, in faith, and in purity. Amen.

Faith

"Faith means being sure of the things we hope for and knowing that something is real even if we do not see it. Without faith no one can please God."

Hebrews 11:1, 6(a)

God, give my children a mighty faith. Amen.

Yearn

"My soul yearns, even faints, for the courts of the Lord; my heart and my flesh cry out for the living God."
Psalm 84:2

Living God, may my children's soul yearn for you; may their heart cry out to you. Amen.

Strengthened Heart

"Strengthen your hearts, for the coming of the Lord is near."

James 5:8(b)

Lord, strengthen my children's hearts and help them be firmly established in your Word. Amen.

Hears and Listens

"Hear the word of the Lord...
Listen to the teaching of our
God."

Isaiah 1:10(a)

Lord, may my children hear your word and listen to your teachings. Amen.

Clear Conscience

"Keep your conscience clear, so that, when you are maligned, those who abuse you for your good conduct in Christ may be put to shame."
1 Peter 3:16

Holy Lord, keep my children's consciences clear so when they are ridiculed for their faith they may stand without shame. Amen.

Declare

"Declare his glory among the nations, his marvelous deeds among all the peoples."
Psalm 96:3

Holy Lord, let my children declare your glory and your marvelous deeds to all people. Amen.

Confidence

"Is not your fear of God your confidence?"
Job 4:6(a)

Dear God, may my children's trust and fear of you be their confidence. Amen.

Desire

"And in any event, you should desire the most helpful gifts."
1 Corinthians 12:31

Father, we know that by your grace we each have a spiritual gift. Guide my children to desire the most helpful gifts and to use their gifts in ministry for you. Amen.

Everything in God's Name

"And whatever you do, in word or deed, do everything in the name of the Lord Jesus, giving thanks to God the Father through him."
Colossians 3:17

Lord Jesus, may everything my children do bring honor to your name. Amen.

Eternal Life

"Take hold of the eternal life, to which you were called and for which you made the good confession in the presence of many witnesses."

1 Timothy 6:12

Jesus, may my children confess that you are their Redeemer and take hold of the eternal life given through your grace. Amen.

Generous

"All goes well for those who are generous, who lend freely and conduct their business fairly."

Psalm 112:5

Help my children, O Lord, be generous, lend freely, and conduct their business fairly. Amen.

Merciful

"Be merciful, just as your
Father is merciful."
Luke 6:36

Father, show my children the mercy
of Jesus and teach them to be merciful
just as you are merciful. Amen.

Fear God

"Happy are those who fear the Lord, who greatly delight in his commandments."
Psalm 112:1

May my children fear you with reverent awe and delight in your Word. Amen.

Speaking Truth

"Speaking the truth in love, we will in all things grow up into him who is the Head, that is, Christ."

Ephesians 4:15

Jesus, let my children speak the truth about the Gospel in love to build up your church. Amen.

Loving

"We love, because he first loved us."

1 John 4:19

Dear Father, we love others because you first loved us. Help my children understand the depth of that love. Amen.

Led by the Spirit

"Those who are led by the Spirit of God are children of God."

Romans 8:14

Holy Spirit, lead my children daily. Amen.

Striving

"And this we labor and strive, that we have put our hope in the living God, who is the Savior of all, and especially of those who believe."

1 Timothy 4:10

Jesus, may my children strive for the life to come through faith in your death and resurrection. Amen.

Living by the Spirit

"... live by the Spirit, and you will not gratify the desires of the sinful nature."

Galatians 5:16

Lord, help my children live by the Holy Spirit's instructions so they follow your way and not their sinful nature. Amen.

Responsible

"For we are each responsible for our own conduct."
Galatians 6:5

Lord, help my children be responsible for their conduct. Amen.

Belonging to God

"The person who belongs to
God accepts what God says."
John 8:47

**Father, may my children belong to
you, hear what you say, and do your
will. Amen.**

Blessed

"Blessed are they whose ways are blameless, who walk in the law of the Lord."

Psalm 119:1

Lord, may my children's ways be blameless, may they walk in your laws, and be blessed. Amen.

Not Anxious

"Do not be anxious about anything, but in everything, by prayer and petition, with thanksgiving, present your requests to God."

Philippians 4:6

Jesus, help my children not be anxious about anything, but in everything, by prayer and with thanksgiving bring their requests to you. Amen.

Vigorous in the Truth

"See that you go on growing in the Lord, and become strong and vigorous in the truth you were taught."

Colossians 2:7(b)

Heavenly Father, may my children keep on growing in their faith and become strong and vigorous in the truth they were taught. Amen.

Act Justly

"And what does the Lord require of you? To act justly and to love mercy and to walk humbly with your God."
Micah 6:8

God, help my children act justly, love mercy and walk humbly with you. Amen.

Respect

"Show respect for everyone."
1 Peter 2 :17

Jesus, please help my children show respect for everyone. Amen.

Strong Grip

"With all these things in mind, dear brothers and sisters, stand firm and keep a strong grip on everything we taught you both in person and by letter."
2 Thessalonians 2:15

Help my children stand firm and keep a strong grip on everything I have been teaching them about your truths. Amen.

Cling to Good

"Hate what is evil; cling to what is good."

Romans 12:9(b)

Almighty God, help my children to hate what is evil and cling to what is good. Amen.

Clear Minded

"The end of all things is near. Therefore be clear minded and self-controlled so that you can pray."

1 Peter 4:7

Keep my children clear minded and self-controlled so they may pray at all times and be prepared for the end times. Amen.

Hold Unswervingly to Faith

"Let us hold unswervingly to the hope we profess, for he who promised is faithful."
Hebrews 10:23

Jesus, strengthen my children to hold unswervingly to the hope they profess for I know you are faithful to your promises. Amen.

No Favoritism

"...as believers in our glorious Lord Jesus Christ, don't show favoritism."
James 2:1

Dear Jesus, as believers keep my children from showing favoritism. Provide them with the ability to lovingly treat all people equally. Amen.

Self-Control

"So we should not be like other people who are sleeping, but we should be alert and have self-control."
1 Thessalonians 5:6

Father, keep my children from spiritual slumber; help them be alert and maintain self-control. Amen.

Patient

"Be patient with everyone."
1 Thessalonians 5:14(b)

Almighty God, help my children to be patient with everyone. Amen.

Pray For Life

"I love the Lord because he hears my prayers and answers them. Because he bends down and listens, I will pray as long as I have breath!"
Psalm 116:1-2

Lord, thank you for hearing and answering my prayers. May my children recognize your faithfulness and pray as long as they have breath. Amen.